HOUSE OF
THREE TURKEYS

This image was discovered in a remote canyon of the American Southwest. There are some of us who wonder if she may have been the last of the Anasazi children.

HOUSE OF

THREE TURKEYS:

ANASAZI REDOUBT

Photographs by DAVE BOHN
Text by STEPHEN C. JETT

A NOEL YOUNG BOOK
Published by Capra Press
1977

Library of Congress Cataloging in Publication Data
Bohn, Dave.
  House of Three Turkeys.
  "A Noel Young book."
  Includes bibliographical references.
  1. Three Turkey Ruins, Ariz. I. Jett, Stephen C.,
1938- II. Title.
E99.P9B57   979'.137   77-15013
ISBN 0-88496-115-8
ISBN 0-88496-115-X pbk.

ACKNOWLEDGMENTS
The authors wish to thank the Parks and Recreation Department,
Navajo Tribe, and especially Charles S. Damon and J. Lee Correll, for
written permission to visit and photograph Three Turkey House in 1972
in order to create this monograph. Thanks also to Clyde Childress and
Mary Jett for assistance in the field. Cooperation of the following
institutions materially aided the research: Brooklyn Museum, Museum
of the American Indian-Heye Foundation, Museum of Northern
Arizona, Navajo Tribal Museum, Northern Arizona University Library,
St. Michaels Catholic Mission, Southwest Museum, Trinity Presbyte-
rian Mission, U.S. National Archives, U.S. National Park Service
(Canyon de Chelly National Monument), University of California
(Davis, Berkeley). The selection by Richard F. Van Valkenburgh is
reproduced from *Desert Magazine*. The map (from Colton, 1939b) was
revised by the writer and redrawn by Rob Kent.

Capra Press
631 State Street
Santa Barbara, CA 93101

For Melissa, Jessica, and Jennifer

PROLOGUE

Why did they leave and where did they go? If asked too often, these questions can become an almost unendurable game. Best to dwell on such matters only briefly unless you have a mind for the utter silences of a canyon night. If so, then by the nearly-full moon Three Turkey House radiates an awareness that seven centuries have slipped by and why have they not come back? And the child? If she *was* the last of the Anasazi children... does she know?

D.B., March 1977

FOREWORD

The face of northeastern Arizona is creased by canyons. Across the piñon-clad Defiance Plateau cuts a winding gorge whose middle reaches are especially twisted and shadowed. On the outside of meanders, shallow caverns have been worn into the seamed, crossbedded sandstone walls. In one of these caves—a sheer fifty feet or more above the rocky streambed—is a silent hamlet, the blocks of its ancient houses flung into frozen composure down a sloping ledge... Three Turkey House, the most perfect small cliff dwelling in the Southwest.

Anasazi—"ancestral enemies"—the Navajo call the vanished builders of these canyon refuges, who once occupied almost all the plateau country. Over the decades, the world has learned of the great sites—Pueblo Bonito at Chaco Canyon, Cliff Palace at Mesa Verde, Betatakin and Keet Seel at Tsegi Canyon, and Mummy Cave at Canyon del Muerto. Relic hunters have plundered, archeologists excavated, and the National Park Service preserved these famous Anasazi ruins, and tourists have now overrun many of them. But in the fastness of Three Turkey Canyon, lying aloof from the attentions suffered by the others, there remains a cluster of eighteen almost perfectly preserved rooms—built seven hundred years ago and forming an unconscious cubist ensemble that makes the spirit of the rare visitor sing.

S.C.J.

PREHISTORY

No one knows who the first inhabitants of Three Turkey Canyon were, but before the beginning of the Christian era pre-agricultural gatherers of wild plants and hunters of wild animals surely threaded their way through the gorge from time to time, in their continual quest for food. Though no positive trace of these nomads has been discovered, it is likely they camped in Three Turkey's more accessible caves.[1]

A few pictographs, some slab-lined storage cists, plus somewhat ambiguous evidence turned up in the archaeological excavation of a cliff shelter suggest that a small community of pre-Puebloan Basketmakers succeeded the hunter-gatherers in the canyon. These people, the earliest Anasazi, presumably cultivated the uplands and canyon floor on a small scale, and supplemented their crops with wild plants and with animals hunted by means of spear and spear-thrower. As yet, no vestige of the Basketmakers' simple dwellings has been unearthed in Three Turkey's cool cliff shelters.

As the middle of the first millennium A.D.

passed, local innovation and the introduction of ideas from the south gradually transformed the Colorado Plateau province's Basketmaker culture into what some call Developmental Pueblo culture. Only a few potsherds bear tangible witness to this way of life in the canyon, but it was certainly present; much more evidence of this culture has been found in nearby Canyon de Chelly. Houses— if any were built in the gorge—would have been more substantial than those of earlier eras. Farming improved during Developmental Pueblo times, and pottery began to eclipse the fine basketry which had characterized the previous period.

The passing centuries saw further refining of Puebloan culture, which culminated, in many ways, during the Classic Pueblo period, A.D. 1100 to 1300. About 1200, a few small structures were built in Three Turkey Canyon. These included a two-story, two-room house in a cave 800 yards down-canyon from the site of Three Turkey House. This residence was burned and abandoned a half century later.[2] It is not known whether the destruction of this dwelling resulted from accident or from attack. However, its end seems to coincide with the arrival of the builders of Three Turkey House.

Architecturally, Three Turkey House appears to be a typical cliff-dwelling in the tradition of the western, or Kayenta, branch of Classic Anasazi culture. However, other evidence strongly suggests that the builders, or at least important members of the community, were Mesa Verde Puebloans from the northeast. This is attested to by the fact that two-thirds of the decorated pottery sherds found there were of Mesa Verde black-on-white styles.[3]

Further, the geometric bands painted on the wall of the ceremonial kiva closely resemble wall paintings found at Mesa Verde, such as at Painted Kiva House. The kiva itself is of the Mesa Verdean "keyhole" plan, although the typical pilasters are lacking. There is abundant evidence of Mesa Verdean immigration at this time in the Canyon de Chelly system, and Three Turkey House seems to be a manifestation of this same movement.

Whether the Mesa Verde people found the canyon deserted when they arrived, or whether they drove out or absorbed the earlier Puebloans, is not known. The immigrants did seem to fear attack, however, choosing not to build in any of the more accessible cliff shelters but in a cave where access was protected by a sheer, fifty-foot cliff wall. Adjacent to the village entryway, they constructed a parapet pierced by a loophole which commanded the difficult ascent.

We can imagine the enormous efforts involved in constructing this eyrie: the men, sweating, nearly naked, hauling tons of rock up a flexing ladder from the canyon bottom below; the women laying the rocks in place, covering them with mortar, and laying on more stones until the walls are head height. The men, who have searched the highlands for straight pines and firs and have carried them to the canyon, now rope the logs up the cliff face to the ledge. They lay the beams at regular intervals from wall top to wall top to support the roofs, which they build of split juniper poles, juniper bark, and a topping of mud smoothed by the small, brown hands of the women.

At last, the houses are completed; the kiva built,

15

plastered, and decorated; and the parapet erected to protect against intruders and to keep young children from falling onto the rocks far below. Life settles into a routine almost timeless save for the daily rhythm and the cycle of the seasons. Each morning, the still air is perfumed by pinyon smoke from breakfast fires. Summer days are passed in planting, hoeing, and harvesting. In autumn, pine nuts are gathered and deer are stalked. Winter is the time of the great ceremonies, which demand hours and days, and in this season, too, utensils and tools are made and repaired. Births, marriages, and deaths are merely parts of the cycle—the daily, yearly, cosmic cycle of Earth, Sky, and their offspring.

Then, something happened to end it all in Three Turkey Canyon. No new building occurred after about 1276,[4] and by the early 1300's Anasazi voices no longer echoed between the sheer sandstone walls. Brush and scrub oaks invaded the cornfields. Deer walked unafraid past the vacant stares of dark doorways looking down from the ledge. Why the people left, no one knows. Perhaps the best guess is that the same enemies who inspired the defensive siting of the cliff dwelling finally made life untenable—not by direct assault on the stronghold but by sporadic raids in the scattered fields, with the theft of crops and the occasional killing of farmers. These raiders may have been bands of Apacheans, recently entered into the Southwest from the north.[5] The surviving Three Turkey people—who earlier may have been driven to the canyon refuge from Mesa Verde—no doubt moved on to other pueblos, in the Little Colorado River drainage. The

16

fugitives were few and were presumably eventually submerged in the host populations, gradually losing their separate identity.

The canyon remained essentially silent for nearly four hundred years, until Navajos drifting westward with their flocks ultimately occupied—though thinly—the entire region. Even today, only a few Navajos use the canyon regularly, and the days of Anasazi village life high on the cliffside have long since disappeared.

NOTES

[1]Olson and Lee (14), p. 76, found charcoal flecks in the fill of one cliff shelter at depths below the lowest ceramic remains.

[2]The above is based largely on Olson and Lee (14) and Link (11).

[3]Colton (4), pp. 28-31.

[4]Colton (3); Smiley (15), p. 25; Bannister, Dean, and Gell (2), p. 32.

[5]Stephen C. Jett, 1964, Pueblo Indian Migrations: An Evaluation of the Possible Physical and Cultural Determinants, *American Antiquity,* 29(3), pp. 281-300.

"Man may scratch the past with his frail stick plow. He may fling himself into the future seeking limits to the limitless sky. He may strut upon a stage too vast for any drama he may make or comprehend. It does not matter. It is the land that holds us here. It is the unrelenting land, this great, fierce, challenging, canyon-gutted mesa-muscled land, which holds us and which gives us space enough to write a life on—and leaves it to us whether we have courage enough and faith to fill the page."

—John DeWitt McKee, "The Unrelenting Land,"
New Mexico Quarterly, 1957

HISTORY

Although Three Turkey House remained relatively unknown to the outside world until the 1960's, occasional visits by Anglo-Americans did occur over the years. However, no one knows who was the first White to see the site. To 19th-century Anglos, and probably to their Spanish-speaking predecessors, Three Turkey Canyon *was* known by name, as Chellecito or Little Canyon de Chelly; but the gorge was, without doubt, seldom visited. One major exception, however, was the expedition of Capt. John Thompson, 1st Cavalry, New Mexico Volunteers. After destroying many of the Navajo peach orchards in Canyon de Chelly in the summer of 1864, on August 7 "I explored this Cañon [Little Cañon de Chelly] for a distance of about 3 Miles— where I came to a Peach Orchard Containing 450 Fruit trees which I had Cut down." However, Thompson did not penetrate far enough to have observed Three Turkey House.[1]

In 1938, Harold S. Colton observed that "Written on the [ruin's] kiva wall was a partly illegible name which looked like W. E. Hilddinn, followed by the date 1898. In another place were the names of S. E. Day, Jr., and C. L. Day, Dec. 16, 1900. No other names were discovered...''[2] The difficult-to-decipher name and date may well have been ''W. E. Hildebrand 1909,'' for that gentleman, in that year, was contractor for the construction of the Chapel of the Annunciation at nearby Chinle.[3] Sam Day, Jr., and Charles L. Day—sons of trader Samuel E. Day—are, then, the first documented White visitors to the site. Charlie Day was operating a trading post at that time, located some twenty miles southeast of Chinle at a place the Navajos called ''Spring Where the Two Lay Together''—only about ten miles from the cliff dwelling.[4] Charlie's brother Sammie was just entering his teens when the brothers made their trek to the ruin, guided by the Navajo Hhata:tli: Ne:z (Tall Singer). They may have photographed the ancient houses,[5] and since they were inveterate relic collectors it is certain that any signficant artifacts they found were removed forthwith.[6]

Richard F. Van Valkenburgh, an ethnologist with the U.S. Indian Service, heard of Three Turkey House in 1934 while doing field work in Canyon de Chelly. There, a Navajo told Van of a ruin he thought had never been visited by a White man—but no hint of its location was forthcoming. Van inquired among his Navajo acquaintances, but it was not until June, 1937, that Ayo:natlnezi, a singer of the Male Shootingway ceremonial, offered to show the ethnologist the way to the cliff dwelling. The expedition had begun as a quest for colored sands to use in ceremonial sandpaintings. The sands were to be found near the head of Three Turkey Canyon.

A dim foot-trail wound through the piñon pine ahead of us. My Indian companions evidently had been over the trail before. Within a half mile we came abruptly to the rim of a deep canyon, gashed in the floor of the tableland over which we had been traveling.

Our path zigzagged down a precipitous sandstone cliff and led to a deserted hogan in a little amphitheater formed by the canyon walls. Surrounding the old Navajo dwelling was a tiny meadow of green and violet beeweed.

Then we climbed out of the canyon on the opposite side and soon came to the place where the medicine men were to obtain their pigments.

The Indians got down on their hands and knees and scraped the colored sands into red and white piles. Then they took flour sacks from their belts and scooped up the pigment and placed it in their bags. . . .

With sacks well filled we took the back trail. The day was warm and the Indians perspired under the heavy loads they were carrying. When we reached the old hogan in the little meadow at the bottom of the canyon we stopped in the shade to rest and smoke.

After a while Ayo:natlnezi took his cornhusk cigarette from his lips and said to me: "Hosteen, hidden around the bend that lies under the red cliff one will find the opening to a deep and narrow canyon which leads to an old cliff house. Few white men, if any, have seen this place. The sun is still high—shall I lead you there?"

I told him I would like to see the cliff house, and

we started immediately. We were soon in a deep and narrow canyon hemmed in by sheer 500-foot walls.

Clumps of mountain oak bordered the bed of the dry meandering wash. Old hogans were perched high on inaccessible and defensible points. Ayo:natlnezi identified these as the homes of his relatives, who as fugitves, had hidden in the canyon to escape the scourge of Kit Carson's Utes and Mexicans in the Navajo war of '64.

The canyon grew deeper and the shadows broader. Springs began to seep out of the banks and small pools of water bordered by lush vegetation replaced the aridity of the upper canyon. High among the cliffs swallows appeared against the sky. The shrill cry of hawks and the grinding of our shoes in the sand were the only sounds to break the silence.

Hairpin turns in the canyon every few hundred feet restricted our view both forward and backward.

The blue sky lay above us in a narrow slit. The trip was becoming dull by the monotony of this limited view and incessant meandering. Ascending a steep wash bank, which stretched our muscles and took our wind, we reached the summit of a low oak-covered knoll.

My guide was gazing toward the top of the opposite wall. I followed his upward glance—and there in a vast cove in the horseshoe bend of the canyon wall was the most perfectly preserved group of cliff dwellings it has ever been my privilege to see.

In the shade of an oak I sat down to study the picture before me. There were 20 houses as nearly as I could determine, built of sandstone slabs. The circular walls of a plastered kiva stood above the cluster of buildings. And there on an upper wall were three turkeys painted in brown and white pigment. . . .

I asked Ayo:natlnezi for his explanation of the extreme defensive measures adopted by these prehistoric tribesmen. He answered:

"These old people whom the wind, rain and lightning destroyed and whom we call the Old Strangers [Anasazi] lived in this country before the Navajos. Only our Gods and Holy people lived here then. Also the Enemy Monsters. These Monsters would come and sit at the base of the cliff and try to charm the old people to come down or catch them when they were working in their fields. That is why they built high in the cliff."

It was difficult to realize that this perfectly preserved cliff settlement was a dead place. Wood smoke should have been coming from the roof vents. Up on the flat mud covered roofs, naked children should be playing. Burden-laden women should be climbing the sheer hand-and-toe trail while little brown men pulled their stone hoes through the growing corn in the fields in the canyon below.

Van's Navajo friend looked on amusedly while the excited anthropologist attempted to gain entry to the cliff house by means of the hand-and-toe holds and with the aid of the rotten oak pole which was leaning against the cliff. After an afternoon of frustration, Van was forced to abandon his efforts to climb to the cave, in which he had hoped to find a treasure-trove of undisturbed Anasazi artifacts.

Over a year later, Van returned to the ruin with a

friend, Harry Chandlee from California, and Navajo interpreter Scotty Begay. They toted 100 feet of rope into the canyon and tried to swing down into the cave from the high ledge above, but the lip of the ledge extended too far out for this maneuver to succeed. New poles were cut for an attempt from the bottom, but this, too, failed. Two weeks later, Van Valkenburgh returned with Soil Conservation Service photographer Milton Jack Snow, but no further efforts were wasted in endeavoring to make an ascent. [7]

Worried lest pot hunters despoil the cliff dwelling, Van reported its location to the Museum of Northern Arizona at Flagstaff. In late October, 1938, he and Navajo singer Sam Tilden led the Museum party to the ruin. Two cars and a truck, loaded with equipment, carried the group from Ft. Defiance to a point near the canyon head, whence a two-mile hike brought them to the site. Ladders were erected, and guyed with ropes. Museum Director Harold Sellers Colton and his companions scrambled excitedly into the ruin, but to their great dismay virtually no artifacts were to be seen other than the superb buildings themselves, and definite evidence of earlier visits was found. Nevertheless, the museum men collected potsherds, took tree-ring borings for dating, and sketch-mapped the site. [8]

Over the years, Three Turkey House was visited occasionally, primarily by local Anglos. When the Navajo Tribe, with the encouragement of Richard Van Valkenburgh, began to take an interest in tourism and the preservation of scenic and historic resources, Three Turkey House was proposed as a potential Tribal Park. In this connection, Martin A. Link, Director of the Navajo Tribal Museum, surveyed the prehistoric sites of Three Turkey Canyon and concluded that the area was indeed worthy of park protection.[9]

—

My first visit to the site was made in connection with my doctoral dissertation project, which involved inventorying the scenic resources of the Navajo Reservation. I came into the canyon alone, by a steep trail. Although in retrospect it was foolish to do so, I attempted to scale the slightly overhanging ledge on which the cliff house rests. My stiff denim pants precluded negotiating the awkwardly placed toe-holds, so I took them off and tried again—and succeeded. I still remember the thrill of discovering the pristine kiva, which I hadn't known about at all until I looked into what appeared to be an ordinary doorway and saw the dimly lit round chamber and the painted decorative band encircling its wall.

As a result of my visit, I recommended that Three Turkey House be protected, and that it be declared a Navajo Tribal Park. Although official Park status has never been declared for the canyon, the Tribe has taken an interest in Three Turkey's potential as an attraction to travelers. The Tribe built a dirt road to an overlook point opposite the ruin, on the canyon's south rim. Here, in 1963, a viewing platform and picnic tables were provided.[10] It is to be hoped that a formally recognized Three Turkey Tribal Park will ultimately encompass this fine canyon and the swallow's-nest village enfolded in its walls.[11]

[1]Jett (8), pp. 373, 378.

[2]Colton (3), p. 27.

[3]Robert L. Wilken, *Anselm Weber, O.F.M.: Missionary to the Navajo, 1898-1921,* Milwaukee, 1955: The Bruce Publishing Company, p. 116.

[4]Frank McNitt, *The Indian Traders,* Norman, 1962: University of Oklahoma Press, p. 250.

[5]Van Valkenburgh (19), p. 13. A photograph of the site in Lummis' (12) album suggests that the Days took the picture and gave Lummis a print. However, a search of the Day photographs at the Museum of Northern Arizona and the Day Collection at Northern Arizona University has not revealed a copy of this photograph. It is possible that it is the work of Father Simeon Schwemburger of the Franciscan mission at St. Michaels, Arizona. Schwemburger was acquainted with the Days and with H.E. Hildebrand. I have not seen this photograph in collections of Schwemburger's work, however.

[6]Wilken, *op. cit.,* pp. 127-128. Most of the Day collections went to the Brooklyn Institute Museum. My examination of the inventory of these collections did not turn up any allusion to Three Turkey House, however.

[7]Van Valkenburgh (18). The published spelling of the singer's name, "Avoo'anlh nezi," has been corrected to Ayo:natlnezi.

[8]Colton (3, 4).

[9]Link (11).

[10]Jett (7), pp. 144-145; Oldendorph (13), p. 8.

[11]*Entry into Three Turkey House is prohibited. Vandalism or removal of materials is punishable by fine and jail sentence under Federal and Tribal law, and rewards are offered for information leading to convictions. The site is patrolled by Navajo Tribal Rangers.*

Moon-silvered walls.
Blackness behind.
Utter quiet, and yet —
Something stirred . . .

—S.C.J.

"The town hung like a bird's nest in the cliff, looking off into the box canyon below . . . facing an ocean of air. A people who had the hardihood to build there, and who lived day after day looking down upon such grandeur, who came and went by these hazardous trails, must have been, as we often told each other, a fine people. But what had become of them? What catastrophe had overwhelmed them?"

—Willa Cather, *The Professor's House*, 1925

30

"In those days we knew far less of them than we do now. They had the charm of stimulating the unbridled imagination. Who were the cliff-dwellers? Whence had they come? Whither had they gone? Many a time imagination has run riot when I have sat perched high on a cliff-shelf, reached with great difficulty, and, perhaps, at the peril of my life, as I have thought of the primitive and long-dead people. Who built these inaccessible eyries? Of course—so I cogitated—there could have been no other reason for the building of homes in such aloof and impossible sites than that of pursuit by cruel, vindictive, relentless and persistent foes, determined to hurry them out of existence. The cat watching for the mouse; the panther stealthily following its prey; the weasel falling upon quarry asleep; the spider weaving its web and confidently awaiting the entanglement of its victim, were all types of symbols suggestive of the pursuers of the harmless, helpless, doomed cliff-dwellers. Then the final scenes of carnage, blood and wanton destruction, when these devoted people were totally destroyed. I pictured the night assaults, the awakened men and terrified women and children, the rush to the ladders, the firing of bows and arrows, the wielding of crude clubs and battle-axes, the casting of obsidian-tipped lances, while women beat the drums and children wailed and yelled in their terror, and shrieked in their pain when wounded."

—George Wharton James, *Arizona the Wonderland,* 1917

"... it is a civilization rendered in earth tones, hued by the soft reds, ambers, rich loam browns, and bleached tans that are the natural condition of this land of wind and sun. Built with the rock and earth that lay readily at hand and hunkered close upon the rock from which they were born, the old cities have weathered well, retreating only slightly, and then only into a more harmonious union with the face of the land. They, like the earth, abide in a quiet strength, a presence that betokens an assurance of permanence..."

—Donald G. Pike, *Anasazi, Ancient People of the Rock*, 1974

34

"What was the spell of this deep fissure in the rocks? . . . It had such a strange sweet dry fragrance, with sage predominating, but with other perfumes almost as clean and insidious. It was as colorful as a rainbow. It changed with the movements of the sun, never very long the same. It had mystic veils of light, rose and pink at dawn, amber and gold at this hour of high noon, and in the afternoon with shadows lengthening, deepening into lilac, purple, black. Then the immensity of the cliffs, the lofty rims, the far higher domes and mesas beyond, the hundreds of inaccessible and fascinating places where only squirrels and birds could rest—these added to the spell. Not a little, too, was the evidence of a wild people once having lived and fought and died here."

—Zane Grey, *Lost Pueblo*, 1927

"The moon was up, though the sun hadn't set, and it had that glittering silveriness the early stars have in high altitudes. The heavenly bodies look so much more remote from the bottom of a deep canyon than they do from the level. The climb of the walls helps out the eye, somehow. I lay down on a solitary rock that was like an island in the bottom of the valley, and looked up. The grey sage-brush and the blue-grey rock around me were already in shadow, but high above me the canyon walls were dyed flame-colour with the sunset, and the Cliff City lay in a gold haze against its dark cavern. In a few minutes it too was grey, and only the rim rock at the top held the red light. When that was gone, I could still see the copper glow in the piñons along the edge of the top ledges. The arc of sky over the canyon was silvery blue, with its pale yellow moon, and presently stars shivered into it, like crystals dropped into perfectly clear water."

—Willa Cather, *The Professor's House*, 1925

"Such magic is thrown about this period, by the wild spendor of the many-colored cliffs from which the squared tops and ruined towers of the cliff villages peer down, that it is difficult to write it into any scheme of tribal evolution. Eagles mewing about the perilous footholds, great trees rooting where once the slender ladders clung! You walk in one of the winding cañons . . . and suddenly, high and inaccessible in the cañon wall, the sun picks out the little windows in the walls amid the smoke-blue shadows, and you brush your eyes once or twice to make sure you do not see half-naked men, deer- and antelope-laden, climbing up the banded cliffs, and sleek-haired women, bright with such colors as they knew how to wring out of herbs and berries, popping in and out of the T-shaped openings like parrakeets."

—Mary Austin, *The Land of Journey's Ending*, 1924

"Separate from that world of present sunlight, they stood in an ancient time. They walked over the roofs of the houses, examining the red sandstone masonry, the adobe mortar, the wattlework of sticks. Through the low doorways they entered dark rooms sharp with the scent of dwelling rubbish; they looked through the small openings that framed bits of the opposite wall of the canyon . . ."

—Frances Gillmor, *Traders to the Navajos*, 1953

42

"All seemed quiet and monotonous, the level plateau unbroken. With the suddenness of most delight it was there before us. We were at the edge of a deep canyon—the earth had opened before us. The upper parts were vertical walls of sandstone, banded buff and brown; lower down, these broke into steep slopes dark with vegetation. This natural grandeur so suddenly revealed was marvellous enough, but there, opposite to us on the far side of the canyon, was a hanging city, a little pale gold city of towers and climbing houses filling a vast oval hollow in the rock. The dark points of the pines rose up to its foot, the immense black shadow of the cave roofed it with a single span, but the fronts of houses and towers were in bright sunlight, all their angles revealed and the doors and windows showing as jet-black squares. It was like an intaglio sharp-cut in an oval bezel. The stone rose sheer above it to meet the forest and then the unbounded blue. It looked so infinitely remote, there across the gulf, so remote and serene in its rock setting, that it seemed like some dream or mirage of an eternal city."

—Jacquetta Hawkes, *Journey Down a Rainbow*, 1955

Its roof rests on two large Douglasfir beams, and it is entered via a hatchway bounded by two long slabs split from a single piece of stone and laid symmetrically along either side of the opening.

—S.C.J.

44

"It was a stupendous tomb. It had been a city. It was just as it had been left by its builders. The little houses were there, the smoke-blackened stains of fires, the pieces of pottery scattered about cold hearths, the stone hatchets; and stone pestles and mealing-stones lay beside round holes polished by years of grinding maize —lay there as if they had been carelessly dropped yesterday. But the cliff-dwellers were gone!

Dust! They were dust on the floor or at the foot of the shelf, and their habitations and utensils endured. Venters felt the sublimity of that marvelous vaulted arch, and it seemed to gleam with a glory of something that was gone. How many years had passed since the cliff-dwellers gazed out across the beautiful valley as he was gazing now? And how long had it been since women ground grain in those *polished holes? What time had rolled by since men of an unknown race lived, loved, fought, and died there? Had an enemy destroyed them? Had disease destroyed them, or only that greatest destroyer— time? Venters saw a long line of blood-red hands painted low down upon the yellow roof of stone. Here was strange portent, if not an answer to his queries. The place oppressed him. It was light, but full of a transparent gloom. It smelled of dust and musty stone, of age and disuse. It was sad. It was solemn. It had the look of a place where silence had become master and was now irrevocable and terrible and could not be broken. Yet, at the moment, from high up in the carved crevices of the arch, floated down the low, strange wail of wind—a knell indeed for all that had gone."*

—Zane Grey, *Riders of the Purple Sage,* 1912

"*Far up above me . . . set in a great cavern in the face of the cliff, I saw a little city of stone asleep. It was as still as sculpture—and something like that. It all hung together, seemed to have a kind of composition: pale little houses of stone nestling close to one another, perched on top of each other, with flat roofs, narrow windows, straight walls. . . .*

In sunlight it was the colour of winter oak-leaves. . . . Such silence and stillness and repose—immortal repose. That village sat looking down into the canyon with the calmness of eternity. . . . I had come upon the city of some extinct civilization, hidden away in this inaccessible mesa for centuries, preserved in the dry air and almost perpetual sunlight like a fly in amber, guarded by the cliffs and the river and the desert."

—Willa Cather, *The Professor's House*, 1925

ARCHEOLOGICAL
PRECIS

Three Turkey House is designated NA1747 and NA3467 by the Museum of Northern Arizona, E:15:11 by the Arizona State Museum, and Ch-10-9 by the Navajo Tribal Museum. The principal remains rest on a ledge presently some sixty or seventy feet above the canyon floor, although the streambed may have been significantly higher at the time of occupancy. Access was presumably by ladder, and was protected by a looped parapet behind the lower portion of which earth fill was placed to create a level platform. The remains of steps, some built of stone masonry and fill, others of logs and fill, lead up the steeply sloping ledge to and between the dwellings.

The plan (p. 56-7) indicates the disposition of rooms in the hamlet. It is not possible to assign functions to each of them. However, one may guess that rooms 1, 2, 3, and 6 were sleeping rooms of a single clan-related extended family sharing not only the large kiva but also storage and cooking facilities in rooms 4 and 5. Rooms 7, 8, 9, and 15 seem also to have been intended for sleeping, with rooms 10 through 13 their storage chambers. Room 16 may have been a sleeping room with an attached storeroom, 17. Room 18, with a curved wall behind and above it, may represent a similar but unfinished two-room unit. Room 14 may have been intended as a kiva to serve the western grouping of rooms, which were perhaps inhabited by members of a single clan-related extended family. Room 5 has a slab-sided bin built against the cave wall, and room 4 has a platform along that wall, on which are what appear to be several shallow, baked-clay hearths; vestiges of smoke-blackening on the cave wall and roof in this room tend to confirm that cooking was carried on here. There is also a clay-rimmed hearth near one corner of the roof of room 3.

All exterior walls are of roughly coursed or, occasionally, uncoursed sandstone slabs set in generous amounts of mud mortar. No doorways and only a few small ventilation openings face in such a direction as to be vulnerable to attackers from below. Exterior doorways, where they occur, are slightly T-shaped, with pole lintels, except in rooms 1 (trapezoidal) and 2 (oblong). The top of the "T" of room 4's doorway was once considerably higher and wider, but much of it was later filled in with additional masonry.

Roof beams span most rooms, and are set into the walls a few courses below the wall tops. Closely spaced poles rest on, and at right angles to, the beams, and are in turn covered with a thick layer of juniper bark. Earth placed on top of the bark sometimes brings the roof level to the tops of the walls, although slab or mud coping may carry the walls slightly higher than the roof surface. A parapet bounds the roof of room 3. Except in the case of the large kiva, most roof beams project from the walls—four or five feet in some cases—and vertical poles rise from the outer walls of rooms 10 through 14. These may have been used for drying meat or produce. Rooms 4, 5, and 9 are roofless, and the roof of room 10 has fallen in (Colton, 1939a, reported two mealing bins and metates on this roof; a metate was noted on the kiva roof in 1972).

Doorwayless roofed rooms were entered by rooftop hatchways, and stone-slab covers for some of these are still to be seen. Some doorwayed and doorwayless rooms have supplemental roof openings, apparently to improve ventilation. The few "windows" in the hamlet presumably fulfilled the same function.

The interior walls separating rooms 7 and 8 and rooms 10 through 13 are made of vertical split or whole juniper poles reinforced with a few horizontal rods; interstices are filled with mud.

The large kiva is perhaps the only perfectly preserved prehistoric kiva in existence. It is enclosed by thick masonry walls, probably with rubble cores. Its roof rests on two large Douglasfir beams, and it is entered via a hatchway bounded by two long slabs split from a single piece of stone and laid symmetrically along either side of the opening. In the innermost portion of the kiva, opposite a ventilation opening in the outer wall, is a broad wall niche, and a hearth with a slab air-deflector is located near the center of the ceremonial room. Encircling the mud-plastered interior wall are two parallel, dot-bordered, white-painted bands from which extend, here and there, sets of three triangles or oblongs.

Room 4 once had a window, which was later filled in with masonry, leaving a niche in the interior wall. Across and to either side of the exterior of the new masonry were painted three ox-blood-and-white designs. These were thought to represent three turkeys by one of Van Valkenburgh's (1938) informants, who had presumably seen them only from the canyon floor. Sam Tilden, a Navajo singer with the Colton (1939b) party, thought them to represent gourds, while a Hopi who saw a photograph of the paintings believed they were clasped hands. None of these interpretations is entirely satisfying. Two buff pictographs of quadrupeds also appear on the rear wall of the cave.

Above and to the east of the main Three Turkey House is a second ledge, on which are found additional architectural remains. One masonry room about eight feet high is well preserved, although its roof has collapsed. Its walls, which have rounded corners, are about twelve feet long (Link, 1959). Two ruined storage structures, using both conventional masonry and vertical slabs, are found to either side of the principle structure, and vestiges of other masonry walls are also to be seen on the ledge.

Numerous small sherds of corrugated and smooth gray utility pottery are scattered about Three Turkey House. The Colton (1939b) party collected a sample, as well as all the decorated sherds, which are classified as follows:

SHERDS OF UTILITY WARES

	No.	Percent
Little Colorado Corrugated	93	43.4%
An Undescribed Rough Pottery	62	29.0%
Tusayan Corrugated	59	27.6%

SHERDS OF DECORATED POTTERY

	No.	Percent
Mesa Verde Black-on-white	40	66.7%
Undescribed Black-on-white	4	6.7%
Tsegi Orange Ware	8	13.3%
Tusayan Black-on-red	2	3.3%
St. Johns Polychrome	4	6.7%
Klageto Black-on-yellow	2	3.3%

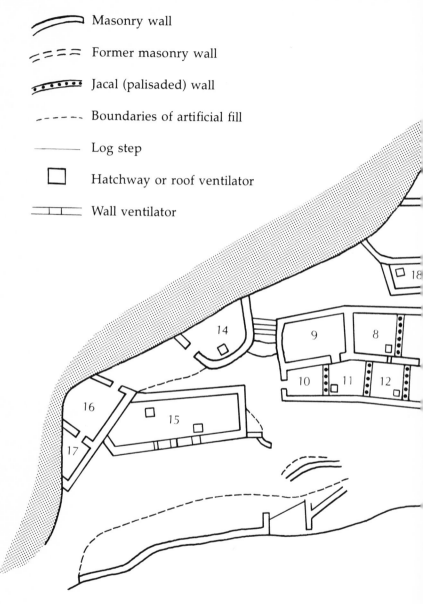

Masonry wall

Former masonry wall

Jacal (palisaded) wall

Boundaries of artificial fill

Log step

Hatchway or roof ventilator

Wall ventilator

56

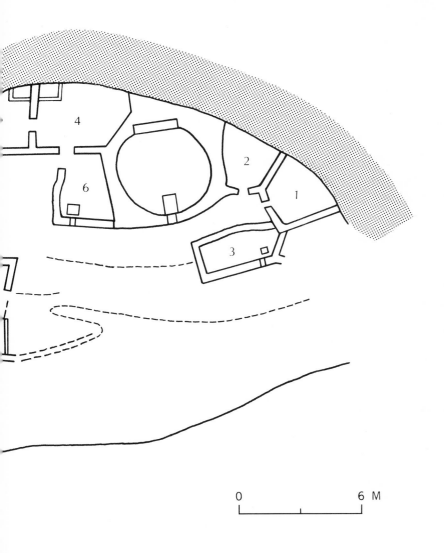

0   6 M

PLACE-NAMES

Van Valkenburgh (1941) gives the Navajo name for Three Turkey Canyon as "Chiih Ḷigaii bikooh, Whitish Red Ochre Canyon," after the ochre-collecting site near the canyon head. More accurately, this would be *Chi:h Tlagai Bakoh*, "Red-Ochre-Is-White Canyon" (or "Watershed"). Place Where Red Ochre Is Gathered, near Canyon de Chelly, is mentioned in the Navajo Prostitutionway legend (Kluckhohn, 1967). The United States Geological Survey quadrangle maps (1955) call the stream "Tse Deshzhaii (or Tse Des Zyaee) Wash," presumably from the Navajo *Tse De:z'ahi*, "At the Rock Point." Names in English that probably derive from Navajo names are "Red Rock Canyon" (Lummis, 1906) and "Red and White Canyon" (Colton, 1939b).

In 1864, Capt. John Thompson called the canyon "Little Cañon de Chelly" (Jett, 1974: 373). The term "Three Turkey Canyon" seems first to have been employed in print by the Geological Survey, in 1955.

According to Van Valkenburgh (1941), the Navajo know Three Turkey House as "Tsenii 'kinni', House High up in the Rock" or, more correctly, *Tseni:'kini*, "At Rock-Middle [ledge] House." He gave as an alternative "Tazhii bikin" (he spelled it "Tatazih bekin" in 1938), "House of the Three Turkeys." *T)hazhi:*, literally "which pecks at," means "turkey"; *bikin* is "its house." Colton (1939b) spelled the name incorrectly, as "Tatalki-Bikin," and used the English appellation "Three Turkey House." The U.S.G.S. substituted "Ruins" for "House."

BIBLIOGRAPHY OF
THREE TURKEY CANYON

1. Baldwin, Gordon C.; David Muench. 1972. Cities of First Americans. *Arizona Highways*, 48(1): covers, end-papers, 16-33, 42. Phoenix: Arizona Department of Transportation.

The cover is a color photograph of Three Turkey House, from the overlook.

2. Bannister, Bryant; Jeffrey S. Dean; Elizabeth A. M. Gell. 1966. *Tree-Ring Dates from Arizona E, Chinle-Canyon de Chelly-Red Rock Area*. Tucson: Laboratory of Tree-Ring Research.

Page 32 gives the date 1266 for a kiva beam, and dates to 1276 for beams in room 15.

3. Colton, Harold Sellers. 1939a. The Date of Three Turkey House. *Tree-Ring Bulletin*, 5(4): 28. Tucson: Laboratory of Tree-Ring Research.

Report on the dendrochronology of Three Turkey House.

4. ___ 1939b. Three Turkey House. *Plateau*, 12(2): 26-31. Flagstaff: Museum of Northern Arizona.

Report of the Museum of Northern Arizona survey of Three Turkey House in 1938, with a description of the site and a report on the ceramics.

5. Coon, John Henry. 1948. The Three Turkey House. *Natural History*, 57(8): 382. New York: American Museum of Natural History.

A brief history of the site, with two photographs of the ruin "by author" (actually by Dr. Thomas Noble, Jr.), one from the trail and one from below and opposite the site.

6. Current, William; Vincent Scully. 1971. *Pueblo Architecture of the Southwest: A Photographic Essay*. Austin and London: University of Texas Press.

Pages 92 and 93 reproduce two of Current's photographs of Three Turkey House, taken from the overlook.

7. Jett, Stephen C. 1967. *Tourism in the Navajo Country: Resources and Planning.* Navajoland Publications, A. Window Rock: Navajo Tribal Museum.

Three Turkey House is described, and proposals for its future made, on pages 144-145.

8. ___ 1974. The Destruction of Navajo Orchards in 1864: Capt. John Thompson's Report. *Arizona and the West,* 16(4): 365-378. Tucson: University of Arizona.

Reproduces Thompson's military report and discusses his route, which included lower Three Turkey Canyon.

9. Kinnear, Willis. 1965. House of Three Turkeys. *Desert Magazine* 28(5): 32-33. Palm Desert.

A description of Three Turkey House as seen from the overlook, with a brief summary of Colton's findings. Contains a photograph of the site, plus a painting of the three "turkeys."

10. Kluckhohn, Clyde. 1967. *Navaho Witchcraft.* Boston: Beacon Press (originally published 1944, Papers of the Peabody Museum of American Archaeology and Ethnology, Harvard University, 22(2), Cambridge).

States (p. 166) that a protagonist of the Prostitutionway legend visits Place Where Red Ochre is Gathered, near Canyon de Chelly.

11. Link, Martin A. 1959. *Report on the Archaeological Survey of Little White House and Three Turkey Canyons.* Window Rock, Arizona: unpublished manuscript at Navajo Tribal Museum.

Describes five minor archeological sites in and near Three Turkey Canyon, plus Three Turkey House itself.

12. [Lummis, Charles F.] 1906. *Photographs, Vol. 5, Gallup, Saint Michael's Ft. Defiance, Ganado, Hubbell's, Keam's Canyon, Chinle, Canyon de Chelly Cliff Dwellings.* Los Angeles: unpublished photograph album at the Southwest Museum.

Photos 185 and 186 are of "Red Rock Cañon Cliff House" (Three Turkey House), from the canyon floor.

13. Oldendorph, O. F. 1964. Three Turkey House. *National Parks Magazine,* 38(203): cover, pp. 3, 8-9. Washington: National Parks Association.

A brief description, plus a summary of Colton 1939b. Includes a map, a painting of the "turkeys," and a photograph of the site taken from the rim.

14. Olson, Alan P.; Thomas A. Lee, Jr. 1964. NA 7696, a Stratified Site in Three Turkey Canyon, Northeastern Arizona. *Plateau,* 36(3): 73-82. Flagstaff: Museum of Northern Arizona.

Describes the procedure and results of testing this site, down-canyon of Three Turkey House.

15. Smiley, Terah L. 1951. *A Summary of Tree-Ring Dates from Some Southwestern Archaeological Sites.* University of Arizona Bulletin, Laboratory Bulletin of Tree-Ring Research, No. 5. Tucson.

Page 25 lists Three Turkey dates from Colton, 1939a.

16. Suplee, Charles; Douglas and Barbara Anderson. 1965. *Canyon de Chelly National Monument, Arizona.* Ganado, Arizona: Suplee-Anderson.

Illustrated pamphlet on Canyon de Chelly; also contains two photographs (pp. 14-15) of Three Turkey House, one from the overlook, one in the ruin itself.

17. _____ 1971. *Canyon de Chelly: The Story Behind the*

Scenery. Las Vegas: KC Publications.

A revised version of the above work. Contains one black-and-white photograph in the ruin, and one color plate (by David Muench) of the ruin as seen from the opposite rim. The site is referred to on p. 24.

18. Van Valkenburgh, Richard. 1938. We Found the 'Three Turkey' Cliff Dwellings. *The Desert Magazine*, 2 (11): pp. 11-13, 37. El Centro.

Tells of Van Valkenburgh's visits to the site. Includes two Milton Jack Snow photographs, of the author and "Avoo'anlh nezi" and of the ruin from below, plus a somewhat fanciful painting of the three "turkeys."

19. ___ 1941. *Diné Bikeyah*. Mimeographed booklet edited by Lucy Wilcox Adams and John C. McPhee. Window Rock: U.S. Dept. of the Interior, Office of Indian Affairs, Navajo Service.

Contains a brief description of the site and the canyon (p. 157).

United States Geological Survey Topographic Maps. 7½ minute-series quadrangles (1955): Chinle 4SE, Sonsela Butte 3SW and 3SE, Zith-Tusayan Butte 2NW and 2NE. 15 minute-series quadrangles (1955): Canyon del Muerto, Nazlini.

This first edition
was printed in October 1977
in Santa Barbara by Haagen Printing
Company and bound by Mackintosh & Young.
Body type is Palatino set by Charlene McAdams,
display type is Albertus, handset by Aaron Young.
Five hundred copies were casebound by Stauffer
Edition Binding in Los Angeles. Two hundred
fifty of these were signed by the
author and photographer.